Hannah and the Monk

JULIA BIRD grew up in Gloucestershire and now lives in London. She works for the Poetry School and as a freelance live literature producer.

http://www.juliabird.wordpress.com

Hannah and the Monk

Julia Bird

To Joy
with best wishes –
Julia Bird

SALT

CAMBRIDGE

PUBLISHED BY SALT PUBLISHING
14a High Street, Fulbourn, Cambridge CB21 5DH United Kingdom

© Julia Bird 2008

The right of Julia Bird to be identified as the
author of this work has been asserted by her in accordance
with Section 77 of the Copyright, Designs and Patents Act 1988.

Salt Publishing 2008

Printed and bound in the United Kingdom by Biddles Ltd, King's Lynn, Norfolk

Typeset in Swift 9.5 / 13

ISBN 978 1 84471 423 0 hardback

Salt Publishing Ltd gratefully acknowledges
the financial assistance of Arts Council England

1 3 5 7 9 8 6 4 2

for four country babies

Contents

Acknowledgements

Acknowledgements are due to the editors of the magazines and websites where some of these poems first appeared—*14, Brittle Star, Limelight, Litro, www.poetcasting.co.uk, Magma, Pen Pusher, Rising, Smiths Knoll, The Wolf.*

Thank you to Arts Council England for its generous support; and to all the friends who have offered advice and encouragement during the writing of this book—particularly and especially Andy.

Article of Faith

Et tu, Brute.
Brutus, even you.
Don't tell me it's not true,
the college city urban myth
that every breath you or I or anybody takes
contains a single molecule of air
expired with Caesar's dying words.
To me it is an article of faith
that my blood, yours and everyone's
is salt with two-thousand-year-old oxygen
and, it follows, grains of every sneeze
or yawn or opera that there's ever been.
Steam from Stephenson's first Rocket ride,
songs that went to space and back,
each bark and war-cry, each World Cup whistle blast,
Spartacus shouting *I'm Spartacus*,
Kirk Douglas shouting *I'm Spartacus*—
particles of these are sherbet in our throats.
And this is where I make observance:
the front row seat in the stalls
for the opening speech of the final act,
at the foot of the soap-box and the busker's pitch
and in the market, where the man who sells fruit
is zesting the air with his citrus patter.
Here, my lungs are nets to catch
this glitterfall of exhalation
to keep with Caesar's sigh and Cassius's kiss.
This cloud of breath's a borrowing and lending
which links everyone, including me and you.
Do you believe it too?
Breathe, if you do.

Jim Fixed It For Me

Every child had a place on the podium
but the gold medal goes to the boy who wanted Jim
to fix to the ceiling above his bed
a full-sized antique chandelier. Which Jim did

though it swung in the room all the wrong scale
like ladies' earrings on a little girl.
The boy's mum, watching from the bedroom door,
was partly proud and partly at a loss

as, unlit, the hanging glass meant nothing more
than dusty test-tubes, foil bottle-tops.
But when the dimmer switch was spun
light, like a slowly forming thought,

started humming in the chandelier's chimes.
Its heart-cut jewels thrilled, and spawned
a rush of sparks—part shoal, part flight—
to moth and mirror-ball the bedroom walls

and bead the boy's school uniform
with sequins, shuntle, mussel pearls;
to lift dark corners of the studio
and drop small sunsets on the audience

till the show was over, the TV set shut down.
For a while, some charge behind the screen
keeps the grey glass platinum, the echoing of light
pinholes the evening through a faint white dot.

Time, Ladies, Please

A woman walks into a bar.
She is not followed by a belly laugh
or a playful punch line to the upper arm.
Rather, she picks a seat where she can see the door,
racks up a trayful of dead and empties—
glasses smeared with blotted kisses—
and plays her own version of beer-mat tricks,
patience and tarot, mats splayed out then stacked.
In the snug, a round of blokes gets the Guinness in,
sloppy flowers dribbled in the froth,
while the shrapnel jackpot shot from the fruitie
is pumped in the jukebox or Durex machine.
In the Ladies' the woman queues, while a girl
mops with bog-roll the dregs of a crying fit
brought on by jealousy or too much gin.
It's in the timing, like the telling of a joke,
the moment between early doors and chucking out
you choose to stand, or be stood, up and go.

The World's Population Visits the Isle of Wight

Belgium is worried it's left the iron on
so even though it's next in the ferry queue
it turns its buses round and heads back home
to check. Denmark is caught up in the traffic
blocking every road and sea lane heading
for the Solent. It's played out a test match
of pub sign cricket and is now sitting silent
in the backs of cars, huffing the windows,
drawing faces and curses in the steam. Japan's
not even left yet, is still in the loft, looking
for its hold-alls, wind-break mallets, beach-balls,
while its taxi for the airport waits.

The man with the clipboard marks another box
on his tick-list as the coaches roll into Cowes.
Four years to plan this task, four flown years
of checking and re-checking, unfiling and filing
the flipcharts and spreadsheets which sort out this 'land,
that 'stan with whatever it is they ought to know
about passports, visas, yellow fever pills. He holds
his piles of paper, paper-clips and clipboard
close and tight. It falls on him to test
that end-of-lesson poser set by every
science teacher: all things being equal, could you get
the world's population on the Isle of Wight?

They fit. There's some doubling up in the B&Bs
but the landladies juggled the kitchen shifts
and keep all day full English on the go—
full Seychellois, full Swedish too. Well fed,
the kids of Mali and Australia
are digging on the beach at Alum Bay.
With spades and castle buckets they have built
sand cities of igloos and wigwams, striped
in gritty shades of mushroom, rose and sage

[4]

such as the locals have never seen before.
The regulars in Shanklin's pubs and bars
can talk of nothing else as they pull in their chairs

so Iceland can get past, pull them in
again for Tuvalu. Venezuela
didn't fancy beers so went to visit
Blackgang Chine; Venezuela's keen
on dinosaurs, wants to photograph
the fibreglass T-Rex's sunny grin.
In a temporary cabin on Portsmouth docks
the man with the clipboard is at his desk, his tea
untouched, tickets and receipts in heaps to his right,
red pens and Tipp-Ex on his left. A draft
of his final report will follow in a week . . .
while the world hangs hollow at his back.

The Camera Never Lies

I drew the blue back-
ground, screwed the
low stool round to a
better height, put two
pounds twenty in the
slot, thought cheese
thoughts and sat for
the half-pint cartoon
of passport headshots
which is now printing.
While I am waiting

a curl in my cowlick
flips over from left to
right, and I wind my
scarf up higher round
my throat. I eat three
mints, and browse a
bit in the paper on a
writer whose memoir
casts in altered parts
those characters once
thought flawed or flat.

A man sneezes spots
of 'flu at me, just as
I turn my head away.
The tic tacs fizz and
sugar rushes through
my heart, while—like
a light-spill in a dark-
room—some reaction
deeper in makes one
cell split apart and
shudder, split again.

The booth coughs and
delivers a brief report:
somebody I once met
but whose ID's now in
doubt. No small wallet
gallery would hang this
portrait, and a customs
officer would stop and
search it. The instant of
an instant photograph
passes by . . . *like that.*

This Much is Almost Guaranteed

Though this time of the year the nights draw in,
they're drawn on by neon—the glowing come-ons
which flourish in the half shade of a winter city:
a bar-sign bottle's constant topping up,
the pink jingle of show-girls on a theatre wall,
their pendulum legs in lights.

Remember, you'll have seen how rain,
if it comes, will nourish this display,
will bring it on to mirrored double blooms.
It rains. A gutter floods its puddles,
the green cross of a pharmacy becomes
a water lily flickering on the spill.

And these lights will rise the same time of the day
tomorrow. That much is almost guaranteed.

Short Film

Finally they let him have a go, from the garage as far as the pave-
ment. Checking the mirror twice, he lowered the handbrake then
freewheeled the twelve-foot slope. Through the windscreen's
frame he could see the porch step, his mother from the waist
down, milk bottles full of air.

Monoglutton

I am so hungry
I could eat a horse.
I am so hungry I could,
as the Irish say, eat a nun's arse
through the seat of an old cane chair.

There's a bee in my bonnet
and it is this:

       my tongue
is already full fat and extra hot,
hand picked and barn fresh—a dish
made from a hundred ingredients
and served to a thousand guests.
Born burbling it was to be born
with a bum trimmed in noodles
and for what I have received
I am truly thankful—

       but
the beetle in my head has a voice
and he's not just talking rice.
It's rice with the cocoa turned right up
till my whole head is boiling away
like pea soup on the hob.

Go cook an egg I say *Get lost*

but this little beetle persists.
He's a linguist, a specialist
with a study full of menus
and a kitchen full of dictionaries
in languages where just one single word
will order up a steak

cooked to the millisecond length you want it
served on the colour china plate you want it
with the sides of chips or mash you want
and your lucky number of peppercorns in the sauce.

Which is why I have the teeth,
these fangs and paving slabs.

I am so hungry
it's like a shoal of fish in my guts
swam round, ate all the food up.

Glossary of Roughly Translated Idiom

Beetle in the head (Welsh)	To be obsessed with an idea
Bum trimmed in noodles (French)	Lucky
Rice (Hungarian)	Idle talk
Turn up the cocoa (Hungarian)	Turn up the volume
Boiling like pea soup (Welsh)	Chattering excitedly
Go cook an egg (French)	Go away
To have teeth / fangs / paving slabs (French)	To be hungry
To have fish swimming around in your stomach, eating all the food (British Sign Language)	To be hungry

White Horse

In a hill field, a horse grows.
His white coat was fallow till the soil

which dressed him like a rug was cleared.
Farmers curry-combed his flanks for brash,

scattered him from hock to mane
with broken stone, and now he's white as mint,

a thousand hands of height, watching
sheep crop the grass in the field beyond his hedge.

If its gate is left unlocked
any horse could bolt. If this one goes,

I'd like to drove him downriver
from paddy-field spring to a dock-stopped mouth

or take him flat out on the tarmac gallops—
hoof prints marking up the motorway,

the slip-roads and the city streets.
There, an artist could busk him out in chalk

on the pavement in front of a tv shop
or he could sway in the tipsy sign above a pub.

Here he is, sprayed in coupé silver
on the plate glass frontage of an office block,

and when it's night, and the clouds go bay
from bouncing back the traffic glow,

here's his relief on the star-blazed sky—
outline cut by paths of satellites,

a low moon his near eye,
his wink, slow-phasing full to new.

Covent Garden

The meeting has run on.
It's late, he's lost, a little bit.
I offer that I'll walk him to the tube
I lodge near here, it's on my way.

I say *'It's great, this route —*
it takes you past a flower stall
that's packing up this time of night.
They flog their stock so cheap it's practically free.'
He holds on while I dither picking daisies
marked at 50p a bunch.

A man sat by the stall is knocking back a can.

'That's Loz' I say. 'His dog is Rosielove.
He told me that his wife fucked off
but he stays here, necks Woodpecker
to take him to a sweeter place.'

Rosielove is champing at a pigeon on the kerb.

'Where d'you stand on city birds?' I say.
'Rats on wings with feet like spat-out gum?
Or do you like their blushing backs of necks
and wonder where it is they lay their eggs?'

Pigeon pairs are roosting on the station roof.

At the entrance
underneath the moon and planes in tiny triangles of sky
he could kiss me as a scrumper steals a plum.
See these lips, would you not say they're like the hips and haws
that fruit in hedgerows when the winter's coming on?

The street is all corners and shine.
Traffic stutters on the clutch
where people wait to cross the road
and each Belisha flash is like a flower
picked apart to calculate
if love is true or not.

Five Years Trying to Win the Flower Show Vegetable Animal Class

Highly Commended: a large baking potato—
    its shape already reminiscent of the humpback whale—
    set on a plate, surrounded by cabbage
    shredded from the centre of the head
    where its waves are tightest.
    Eyes for a blowhole, and also for eyes.

Highly Commended: a crocodile
    in cucumber, sliced out wedge
    for a gaping mouth, radish teeth and feet,
    and winding down its curving spine,
    a double crest of battlements, contrived
    from cocktail sticks and arrowheads of swede.

Highly Commended: a glossy purple eggplant
    as the body of a bird of paradise,
    wings from tiers of rocket, mint and carrot tops,
    comb from sprouting mustard seed and dill.
    Beak a nutshell, tongue a nut,
    side-dish of summer fruits, its song.

Third Place: the coconut gorilla.
    A corn dolly armature whose stooky thighs
    and sloping head are covered
    in the cracked off shells of coconuts,
    the pile of the coconut fibres
    precisely matching the nap of gorilla pelt.

Highly Commended: an aquarium of fish.
    Goldfish, guppies and angelfish whittled
    from melons, peaches and artichokes.
    Highly skilled engraving suggests drift and flurry,
    fins and scales. A year's work wasted on the system
    to blow bubbles fat as berries from their mouths.

As the Peacock

As the peacock dives towards a lake
to beak a fish up out into the air

and the osprey resting in the carving dish
is butter-balled and basted, stuffed and roast;

as the chicken zips from flower to flower
to drink each optic dry of cordial

and humming birds, like light through coloured glass,
flicker across rough-cut flags of ice;

as from a hanging one-hoof coconut
the penguin, upside-down, pecks crumbs

and the sparrow spreads his blue enamelled tail
on guard outside the harem's gate

so the metal speckles in my skull
align along the hidden iron rails
which take migrating birds away from home.

Paper Stars

What do my paper stars predict?
    The pair of fish, in the rock-pool formed
        by tides of headlines ripping in and out,

has put me on hold for a tarot reader
    whose truth, expressed in spreads of Lovers
        is: cross her palm with today's special offer

for a reading of the lines on mine.
    A biro to-do list, a number to phone,
        both life-line and the heart-line thrown

for comfort, sweetness, tea. Outside the cup,
    the willow pattern movie on a loop.
        Inside, the fallen leaves take the shape of a book—

a Bible, novel, firearms catalogue
    from whose raffled pages I will pick
        the phrase which exposes the one true knack

of sure-fire divination: a magpie count,
    a crystal ball, the runes. They all direct
        the question—what do my paper stars predict?

Short Film II

The supermarket checkout girl at till two smiled at him as he queued and paid for his Mars Bar. Her hair was as black and her lips as red as its wrapper. How 60p in change feels like a divorce.

From Cramond Beach

FRONT

This seascape is an exercise in shades of blue: sky, pure pigment,
airbrushed onto backlit glass, its finish flawless, high.
And the sea, trying to do what the sky tells it to,
makes each wave a version or a cromalin—blue-green a near miss,
grey-blue a rough guess—collaged at the outline of the shore.
Shingle on the beach is Wedgwood. It's fine-ground sherry bottle,
swimming pool tiles, and is stamped with skipping footprints—
a hallmark the length of this transmuted golden mile.

BACK

Am here on the best beach—
made of so much
smashed up mussel shell
the dunes are streaked with blue.
My castles turn out
with that Square Mile, City glitter—
1,000 windows throwing light.
Weather is lovely.
The weather here is lovely.

Fire in a Crowded Theatre

A jaded usherette tells me.

For her own quick ovation, she tells me

'If you're ever in a theatre
and you hear a voice announcing
Mr Jet is in the dressing room
that's code.
      The theatre's code
for us to clear the house, and fast—

It means *Get Out! By Christ!*

*Don't tell the punters but
the dressing room's on fire!'*

She's caught me at a point
when I am tinder, so I see exactly

the lit ciggie set too close to the spirit gum
      for the second act moustache.

Their dialogue. The two beat breath

and the sticky flame which treacles off the table

and into a wicker skip
of doublets, hose and tennis whites,
how it rhubarbs to itself a while then roars—

the heat so fast and loud it blows the light bulbs
round the mirror, one after the other,
a pyrotechnic chorus line of pop and shatter.

I hear the fanfare of smoke
blown under the dressing room door,
which proclaims fire's
        bit of business in the corridor,

        it knocking up the Green Room, Wardrobe, Props:

Ladies and Gentlemen, this is your five minute call

        then see it beat them all into position
see it chafing in the wings,
        shinning up the ropes, across the lighting rig
and dropping burning roses on the stage.

And the leading man here is the stage hand who,
        picking up a dropped cue,
shouts all those behind the curtain out,
        blocks in a crowd scene in the theatre yard
of sooty understudies, dazed and half-dressed stars

who now can see that fire is the plot of this play
        which is also cast with fire. Fire rehearses
and directs, is lighting states and sound effects.
        Fire on stage watches fire in the stalls
and at the climax, when the safety curtain falls
        fire is cheering, clapping.
                Fire is cat calls.

        And later I read the reviews:

        the fly-tower beams
are banner headlines on the sky,
this performance scoring four red engines
        out of five.

Perhaps the usherette
and I will scuff through the debris,
damped down, cool with one another,

each aware that she had got her lines by heart—
Fire in a crowded theatre our shout—
but equally aware she did not have the skill
to pace a speech, to weigh a pause, to make
an audience sound its beating pulse above the hush.

There's not much limelight in a dim red torch.
Notices are served. The theatre is dark,

its gilt and plush transformed to piles of ash.

Your Grandfather Would Have Wanted You to Have This

So raise a glass of the whisky that was sunk
that this bottled boat could draw a schoonerful
of model sea, to the man who modelled it:
who teased each wave from putty and oil paint
through the keyhole of the bottleneck, who spent
all winter in the dry-dock of the dining room
ship-building a spillikin keel with hair-pin ribs,
who flocked the bottle's concave glass
with flake-of-salt-sized gulls, whose fingers
were made delicate by the tweezers and the button-hooks
it took to tat the rigging, gather-stitch the sails.

No champagne smashed at this ship's launch
but in the cross-trees of its mizzen mast
see, aloft, the balsa wood Ship's Boy
with his minute jeroboam? In that bottle,
your grandpa said, the smallest tot of sea.
On that sea, a fleet.

I Really Should Quit, But

What I'd miss the most
is not the Rizla origami—
that little bit of handicraft
which every time I watch
I think this time it will
turn out a paper swan—

and not the hushing inhalation—
Tell me again how it kicks
like a good cup of coffee
but calms like a mug of hot milk—
the answer in a stream of smoke,
a baffle of personal fog.

I'd miss the odd times in between—
the times when I do have a light
and its spun flint throws out sparks
like a top taken off in the dark,
when my thumb has its small accelerator
floored, the moment when
the flame takes hold

and the distance between us
is king-sized, and blazing.

Opinion

Please look at these x-rays a moment,
perhaps they'll show you what I meant.
With his skeleton flaring like a filament

and his insides lit, you'll see
that at certain points in his history
he broke every bone in his body.

When he fell off his bike
his spine snapped like a buckled snake;
limbs: old dog-toys and drum-sticks.

Skiing dropped the cups and saucers
of his skull and pelvis—
even that rattle of screws and washers

deep in his inner ear
got cracked. They all healed—
each rib and knuckle has a seam—

but I'm trying to tell you the scars
are starting to give, new fractures
holding only with a flour and water paste.

There are areas of unregenerated loss.
Here, a structure like a pool of milk.
Here, a January sky about to snow.

Magnetic Translation: poetry one one sex

Let me not to the boy-girl-melt of good selfs
say die. Heart-fire is not heart-fire
which changes when it change sees,
or breezes with the cut-brother to cut out.

O no! It is a deep needle picture
that looks on air-fevers and is never blind;
it is the star to every two-go ing fish-above,
whose magic's a question, though his vastness be asked.

Heart-fire's not time's fool, though red lips and blush-pools
within his cut steel circle come;
heart-fire changes not with his green days & times,
but sails it out to the lip of the ocean.

If this be speak-lie, & up on me hard-put,
I never word-worked, or no heart ever fired.

by Will-I-am Cake-star

Short Film III

The elevator's arrival pings an overture. Muzak from basement to penthouse as one passenger reflects in the elevator mirror, each twitch a step in a dream ballet *pas-de-deux*.

The Animals Went in Two by Two

The finch is hardly even winged
in the dogfight with its double-glazing twin
and would—with a minute's fluster on the deck—
flight-check itself and take back off
to circle the garden, then skip the surface
of the pond as if both duck and drake.

Instead, a boy is launched from indoors
who fishes the bird up and press-gangs it,
with biscuits and a drop of water in a lid,
into a shoebox which he beaches on a shelf
above his bed and puts on watch
a crocodile of plastic dinosaurs.

He can't know why the bird won't eat.
All we can do is urge his mother in
to raise the blinds and flood them both with light,
to say—as mothers should—
Why don't you two go and play outside?
Such a shame to waste this sun.

Next Door Girl

We told her: *'Durrbrain.*
There's no such thing as rabbit farms.
Mister Bun's not gone to live on any rabbit farm.
Your dad dug him in round the back of the shed.
We saw him when you were out dancing
at Brownies and he told us not to say.
We dug him out—here, d'you want to smell?'
And we thrust at her a Tesco bag
of chicken bones, spaghetti hoops and soil.

Its name was Rabbiting: the game to play
when football after school was off
or when the telly broke, the holiday it rained.
Its rules were: having her to tea
then eating lettuce at her; getting the thing
for scrubbing pans to stick to the back
of our shorts and whispering
'We learnt a word today.
Shall we tell you? *Scut.'*

We go funny when we think of her:
the way her eyes are white around the brown,
her teeth, her twitchy nose.

Spiv

I often hold the door for them,
sometimes give my seat to old examples on the tube.
The once, I even helped a man on with his coat,
a thin summer thing he'd slung just so
on the back of a pub chain chapel chair.
The point at which we had a sleeve apiece
its front fell undone like curtains parting
at the top of a scene, and there,
pinned like medals to its silk-style lining
were two dozen gold watches, real gold,
fully wound, their mechanisms pittering.
Furthermore, the jacket pocket chimed
with tiny vials of scent. Musk distilled to syrup drops,
and the whole of the hem on the inside of the coat
was trimmed with carefully-packeted nylons.
Nylons. And why would I be wanting nylons
when no one has worn them for forty years?

Clip

Two kids are necking, Americanly,
in the front seat of a Cadillac . . .
a Buick . . . some long red soft-top classic.
The camera picks up on one ten-gallon bee
drumming its feet on the hot tin hood
then pulls out along the buffed upholstery
and hand-waxed body-work.

On the sound-track, a droning thunderhead
of scrubbing strings played bass and indistinct
is a murmur, a rumour of trouble

but back in the front seat,
he flexes, she rocks—and knocks her hip
on the button of the horn which stays on
and stays on. No matter how they giggle,
fumble under the dash, sort
and redress their rumpled state,
the horn keeps calling its one clear note—

a noise the by-now killer bees can't bear.
It angers and confuses them,
primes and blows them like a charge of shot
which zooms in on the road, the classic car,
the kids—and blacks out the windshield,
censors mirrors, blocks the tail-pipe,
vents, their sounding mouths

till a swarm of stock footage,
cut and spliced with cheap FX,
stings and stings the kids to death.

Poor peach-fed kids, to be judged
and sent down by such a buzzing Moses.
If there is to be a sequel, lead the bees
to a local multiplex and lock the doors.
Screen them feature after feature—
nature films of orange groves and orchards
where smoke in the trees is just blossom
where work is the raising of pollen
and all these things are sealed in honey,
the one, the only law.

Hannah and the Monk

'Such a bleating in the bar on market days
when the farmers come to blather about meat
and grazing it, to barter ram for wether
and trade in remedies against the bloat.
I pour the beer and chat and count the pots
while the regulars woolgather, or sit and doze.'

    A thermal chilled. Elmer's faith
    in his angel jackdaw outfit faltered
    and he fell, was earthed in a breathless knot
    of goose-quills, wax and struts.
    His wishbones snapped—but will knit
    enough to bear a tail, another flight.

'When time's been called, I visit the tiger
who's caged in the square, gaze through the bars
as he bothers an entire leg of lamb,
and I listen for the roar. His fur is rough as coir—
or flocked, like a scrap of velvet trim.
That coal-fire coat will either burn or warm.'

    Whether or not you head for the roof
    to throw yourself like dice, or flutter your life
    on a tiger's touch is a long shot, an unshown hand.
    If the risk pays off, you hear the purr of feathers
    in the wind; between the high stakes of the air
    and the stacked odds of the ground.

Radio at Night

When sleep won't stop a dripping tap,
won't warm your feet or keep the burglars at bay,
the radio at night is here.
Radio at night is populous
with plays and sport and life insurance ads,
the radio's a place where Parliament
is passing laws, where orchestras
play lullabies and local DJs host a quiz
where every caller wins a prize.
Pirates rig their decks in tower blocks
to buffet you with heart-shake bass
and taxi drivers, when the sky is clear,
crackle, book a pick-up, fade.
The weather voice, unwavering, avows
there will be rain but it will pass; then
live on air a band begins to play, unplugged,
a song of buckled love set right so sweet
you slow dance from the ankles down.

Count the stations, number off the staff
it takes to play the tunes, to speak the lines,
to talk and comfort the insomniac.
To pause and check each channel on the range:
it feels tonight like gathering in the flock.

Short Film IV

In the kitchenette, a riddled dishcloth fell against the live kettle lead. Electrically ensouled, the resident bacilli began to plot.

What I Would Like is a Birdcage

Vintage. A Victorian mahal of bars
and twisted wires with annexes
and finials intricately engineered
by an Isambard Kingdom birdcage builder.

The type that hung in a parlour, home for a parrot
with a big grey bastard disposition:
a screwed-up list of demands who itched
for a solitary flight through the thick macassar fug

of nineteenth century family life, who told us
himself how *Polly wants a cracker*
as he splintered with his Swiss army foot
the stripes on a dinner of sunflower seeds.

Would I put a bird in it? No.
A radio, maybe, or spider plants
so its bars could profuse with shuffled tunes
or choruses of spiderlings.

I'd like a birdcage to the extent
I almost find it in myself
to *be* a birdcage. Spring these ribs apart
and here are cuttlefish: two scoops

of toasted air, and a red canary
peeping for them on a swing.
Almost. Let's hope it doesn't come to that
nor that you find this cheeky. I did ask nicely

but give much thought to the matter
of gifts I'd like and who I'd like them from.
An empty birdcage. Brass. Please.
Perhaps if I drew you a picture?

Dedication

with love

he wrote

and just what

what am I supposed to make of that

that phrase whose

hackle-raising inexactitude

conveys identical amounts

of near-as-dammit nothingness

as if I had have said

the shirt he chose was green

spearmint

Lincoln

British racing

bottle, olive, pea?

Souchong Sevenling

On a silver salver: a porcelain cup
and saucer, a tea-plate with a doily unique
as a snow-flake. On it: two pastries, one cake.

A cake whose gold-leaf frosting's set—*so*—
with dragées and angelica,
waiting for the one guest still to show.

Past four already and the lapsang stewed.

Supersize Sevenling

I like Big Macs with cheese, small fries.
No pickle please— those bitter bottle tops—
have them picked out. Less ice with this Coke.

I like to tie knots in the paper trousers off my straws.
I like ketchup more than BBQ sauce.
I like McMilkshake girls to sport three stars.

Sweet particulars! he says.

Orange Pips

For years I wore a pin-stripe camouflage:
no time for anything but overtime.
While others put their lovers on parade
outside my office fortress, I'd just watch.

What the nets and leaves were meant to hide
were scars from when the blunt words cut like knives,
disguise the skew-set breaks, and keep from show
the parts of me patched up with metal plates.

Perhaps I might have met my match in you
who, bruised to sweetness, keep your guard
up tree-top high. Do they now rest with me,
decisions about risk and playing safe?

Or should I put this question to an orange?
The tinker's tin-pan heart, the soldier's purple.

Magnetic Translation : come, games 1

The ice-time drunk-day couches up
with in-bits of snacks in crowd-throughs.
Cocktail time.
The hangovers of smokey days.
And look a wiggle pour decorates
the sloppy pinches
of stained drops under and on your boots
and influencers from no-crowd-throughs;
the pours punch
on no-go light-to-nights and smoke-don'ts,
and at the kiss of the big-crowd-throughs
a want-so make-drive is always and never.

And then the call-on of the lights.

by To Es All-he-ate

Short Film V

The stranger kicks open the doors of the pasty shop.

we could nick a boat /
and sneak off to this island

Midsummer at this latitude —
we never get the short, short nights,
the white nights
where the sun is knocked back
and re-filled
in the time it takes to sink a round.

Still, some kind soul has planned
a party for this longest day —
a town-house party
of peanuts in a fingerbowl,
of small, dry white songs on the stereo.

One of the guests is wearing
such shoes — royal blue
rocking-horse platforms
in crocodile patent
with grosgrain ribbon laces.
She has glitter in her crow's feet
and carries about her
the air of burnt letters

and says *Well.*
Whatever am I to do
about this party?

In through its back door
comes the sound of the harbour —
gulls, and halyards glockenspieling
as the tide swells.

But They Wouldn't Want Us to Go Hungry

I watch him tip his long neck back
and ease a tuck of ham, an eighth of fig
from the point of a cocktail stick. A sword swallower. I applaud
        the trick

        then he butters me the torn half of a brown bread roll,
        clicks the waiter over, orders a bottle of his usual.

Two rainbow trout on whiteware plates—
his swimming for the water jug, mine towards the salt.
The horoscope tonight leaves little room for doubt.

        The lamb comes rare in the centre, the outside seared,
        and it all but slips through the bars of his fork as I lean to take
                my share.

Sacher torte reveals its treasure in the mouth,
comes with cream or ice-cream if that isn't rich enough.
Which of you has never wanted, just the one time, both?

        Sugared with freckles, his wrists and the backs of his hands.
        They sweeten the taste of a dark roast blend.

The bill is dutched, the coats are fetched,
but on the rucked up tablecloth there's one glass left.
That final drop of port has whirlpools at its depths.

Duet

for D&L

A bird sang.
King of the castle in the crown of a tree,
the bird made cockadoodle calls to toast the dawn:
at dusk, he cast his songs like spells
to lull the roost to sleep.
He'd sing the story of his life—an air about the sky,
an aria on wings, tunes for following the sun—
but mostly he sang of the young in spring
in hymns to the girl who lived nearby.
Hear-this-love sang the bird.

She heard
and she hoarded the music from the trees,
the birdsong do-re-mis, the trills and tremolos
and the long, low notes, like gold;
told them over and over till,
in a sudden spree, her voice joined his
and the harmony she sang was *yes.*
The notes of their duet will rise and break
like bubbles through champagne, and rain back down
as rose petals, or a shower of rice, or grace.

Pure Maths

Measure a man
between his outstretched middle finger tips.
If he's six foot tall, he'll have a six foot span,
a correlation which applies to everyone.
Measure the man who first worked out this sum,
who would have had the hunch some time,
have sized people up from a way away,
squinting and tilting his head, a pencil—
stylus even—tapping on his chin.

He'd have lined up all his friends,
chivvied them to reach out tall and straight
like simple stars. *Watch me test this new hypothesis*
with nothing more than quadrant, string and rule—
whatever means it was he would have used.

The tension and relief as proof came after proof.
John, you're the same across as up and down,
this many cubits and a barleycorn. Mark,
you also match from head to toe and side to side.

And the notes he would have made on wax tablets—
napkins, even—let's say he took them home
and gave them to his wife as she had
always given him her best belief. *My lofty love*
he would have said. *We correspond.*
We combine in many planes our equal heights
and depths. The maths is pure, and complex.

Breathing Pattern

That window has shifted in the night.
And dark blue daylight borders the blind

but dawn must be on hold:
it took the clock an hour to flick from four

to four oh nine, its winking figures
marking time where no time passes.

Who moved the window? Who made this bed
whose bedclothes fit like they were tailored?

The untucked covers match the dress
I modelled for a short three-hour stretch,

an evening dress whose cinched-in waist
and strapless top made even mirrors stare.

At this hour, no-one stirs. I'm not sure *who*
or, woolly-headed, *where*, but know

I fell here like a feather would—
freely, no fear of the ground—

and touching down, am made secure:
a feather with a flight path in its curve.

The homespun logic of the half-asleep
has tomorrow holding to this new-found shape

if, drifting off, I make my breathing pattern fit
the zip / slow unzipping of his.

Picture Book for Urban Babies

What do pigeons say, baby?
    What do the pigeons say?
The pigeons say 'Croo *croo* croo *croo*
    Flappadaflappadaflap.'

And what's that sound from underground?
    It's the tube trains calling 'Minda GAP
hold tight and minda GAP!'

What do the sirens say, baby?
    What do sirens say?
Sirens say 'Woo woo woo AAANNKH'—
    that's what sirens say.

So what say the geezers who sit in the boozers?
    'I love you, my basin of gravy,
my trouble, my teapot lids.'

What do tourists say, baby?
    What do the tourists say?
The tourists say 'Clickaclickaclicka Gee!
    Clicka Gee! Clickaclickaclicka Gee!'

And what about this great-grandfather clock?
    He's chiming 'Heerizda NEWS
Bong Bong—Heerizda NEWS.'

What do the cafés say, baby?
    What do cafés say?
The cafés chatter 'Mocha Chocha
    Chocha Latte kssh kssh prbprprblprbprpkssh.'

Then what news from the river?
    The grey brown river stays shtum
but will float you and carry you home.

Notes

MAGNETIC TRANSLATIONS

'poetry one one sex' and 'come games 1' are translations of Shakespeare's 'Sonnet 116' and T.S. Eliot's 'Preludes 1' using the vocabulary of the fridge magnet poetry kit, Standard and Party editions respectively.

HANNAH AND THE MONK

Elmer was an eleventh-century monk who flew from the roof of Malmesbury Abbey in Wiltshire dressed as a bird. Hannah Twynnoy (1670–1703) is buried in the Abbey grounds. She was a local barmaid, legendarily mauled to death by a tiger from a travelling menagerie.

WE COULD NICK A BOAT / AND SNEAK OFF TO THIS ISLAND

. . . is a line from Björk's 'There's More to Life than This' from her album *Debut*.

PICTURE BOOK FOR URBAN BABIES

The Cockney rhyming slang is . . .

Basin of gravy—baby
Trouble [and strife]—wife
Teapot lids —kids